robin layton

Dedicated to all the 12s™

FOREWORD

The most amazing thing to me about the Seahawks fans is how loyal they are. Regardless of the win-loss record of the team, they are always there, always shouting, always supportive of their team. Whether the team swept to the Super Bowl or finished in last place, the fans have always been loyal, since day one.

As a player, you form a bond with the fans and you want to play as hard as you can for these people who are so loyal and supportive of the team.

In recent years, Seahawks fans have become a story and a force of their own. "The 12s" provided a thunderous backdrop to the Seahawks' march to back-to-back Super Bowls—and an NFL title in 2014. Their deafening roar gave wing to the Hawks, sent opponents reeling, and rallied the entire Pacific Northwest community.

Look around Seattle today and you'll find 12 jerseys everywhere. 12 flags fly from the Space Needle, office windows, passing cars, homes, and schools. Church reader boards embrace the 12s. Seahawks fans have become known locally as 12s. The photos they take and share of themselves are called "Twelfies."

An honored guest raises the 12 flag before every home game, igniting a crowd frenzy that the team feeds upon. The tradition of the 12 flag began on October 12, 2003 when 12 original season ticket holders hoisted the flag prior to kickoff. From former Seahawks greats to local celebrities and sports personalities, being called upon to raise the flag has become a civic honor. I had the thrill of raising the 12 flag myself in 2003, an experience I'll never forget.

"The 12th Man" has a long and storied role in Seahawks lore. With the birth of an NFL franchise in 1976, Seattle fans were no longer starved for their own professional football team. As the Seahawks prospered, their loud, sold out crowds became known as the 12s. Seattle fans had such an impact on the success of the team in the 1980s that Seahawks President Mike McCormack retired the number 12 jersey on December 15, 1984.

The 12s became an even bigger force when the Seahawks moved to CenturyLink Field. The deafening crowd has wreaked havoc on opposing offenses—forcing more than two false starts per game on average. On November 27th 2005, in a dramatic overtime Seahawks victory, the visiting New York Giants were penalized for 11 false starts. The Giants were so rattled by the crowd noise they also missed three field goals. Coach Mike Holmgren dedicated the game ball to the 12th Man. The ball now resides in the club level at CenturyLink Field.

On January 8, 2011 Seahawks fans literally shook the Earth during the NFL playoff game against the New Orleans Saints. CenturyLink Field erupted with excitement during the 4th quarter when Marshawn Lynch made an astonishing 67-yard touchdown run, broke half a dozen tackles, put the Seahawks up 41-30 over the Saints—and triggered a minor earthquake that registered on a nearby Richter scale.

On December 2, 2013, at CenturyLink Field, against the New Orleans Saints, Seahawks fans registered a decibel reading of 137.6, setting a record for the loudest outdoor stadium in the world. That record comes and goes, but opposing players will tell you that CenturyLink is the most intimidating place to visit in the NFL. The 12s are the reason why.

Robin Layton's photographs in this book capture the passion, energy, and the creativity of the shared community of fans, and raise this passion to high art. Her images are impressionistic and not of this world. They pulse and vibrate and bounce with excitement, evoking the 12s themselves, the best fans in all of football.

— Steve Largent,
Former Seahawks wide receiver,
Pro Football Hall of Famer

" The 12s have an unparalleled impact on game days."

— Pete Carroll,
  Seahawks head coach

" The most amazing thing to me about the Seahawks fans is how loyal they are. Regardless of the win-loss record of the team, they are always there, always shouting, always supportive of their team. Whether the team swept to the Super Bowl or finished in last place, the fans have always been loyal, since day one. As a player, you form a bond with the fans and you want to play as hard as you can for these people who are so loyal and supportive of the team."

— Steve Largent,
Former Seahawks wide receiver,
Pro Football Hall of Famer

" Since the very first day, the very first game of this franchise, the fans have been unbelievable, long before they were called the 12s. The Seattle fans waited a long time to get NFL football here and they cherished it once it came. They have supported it ever since, through really good times and some pretty tough times. Now that the Hawks are one of the top teams in the league, it just gives them even more to cheer for. The fans are spectacular and they can make a difference in a game. There's no question about it."

— Steve Raible, Former Seahawks wide receiver; radio play-by-play voice of the Seahawks

"Being a Seahawks fan, along with the relationship I have enjoyed with the team, has given me the opportunity to be part of a larger community. I've met so many good friends through the Seahawks and through the Sea Hawkers Booster Club activities. My life would be so much different without the team.

Sharing a common goal or bond with so many has really helped me get through some tough times over the past 15 years. It's allowed me some great friendships which otherwise wouldn't be there, and truly improved my quality of life."

— Neil "Kiltman" Hart, Seahawks superfan

" I grew up in Olympia, Washington, but now live in Denver, Colorado. Even though I moved away 30 years ago, I've been a season ticket holder for 20 years.

I fly to Seattle for every home game and usually go to a few away games every year. A lot of guys have a man cave but I have a man house.

It doesn't matter where I live, Seattle is always my home. I've lived in Denver, Oakland, and San Francisco but I've always been a Seahawks fan. I will always be a Seahawks fan. No one can ever take that away from me."

— Paul "Bernie Hawk" Gates, Seahawks superfan

" Seahawks fans are fanatical, knowledgeable, and they come to the stadium on a mission to be completely disruptive to the opposing team. It doesn't matter who Seattle's opponent is. I would venture to guess that of the eight home games Seattle plays each year, the fans are worth four wins to the team. And that says a lot. I've talked to opposing players who've indicated, no doubt, Seattle is the most difficult place to play in the NFL."

— Kenny Easley, Former Seahawks All-Pro strong safety; 1984 NFL Defensive Player of the Year

"Our fans give us that extra energy on game day and are with us through thick and thin."

— Jon Ryan, Seahawks punter

"If you're a fan, you support them win, lose, or draw. You don't just support them when they are winning. I've been a fan since 1976. As long as I can still hoop and holler, I'll be a fan. I love the Hawks. I've been around through thick and thin and now it's the fun years. I doubt if you will ever get a picture of me with my mouth shut. It's a family thing. When we play away games, our family room is full of the kids, the grandkids, and the great-grandkids. My family bleeds blue and green. We have blue and green carpeting in our house. Being 85, it takes a little longer to put my war paint on. When I put that paint on, it's better than Botox because the paint's so stiff I can't close my eyes. I look really good during the game but when I take off the war paint, watch out. I've met most of the players and when the older players come back they always say to me, 'Are you still here?' I say, 'Well, yeah, as long as I'm on this side of the dirt, I'm going to be down here cheering for the Hawks. That's what I do best.'"

— Patti "Mama Blue" Hammond, Seahawks superfan

" We got married on the 50-yard line (the only ones to ever do so) in the Kingdome in September, 1998. The Sea Gals and Blitz, the mascot, were there. Mama Blue was in our wedding and her son married us. That's how we became Mr. and Mrs. Seahawk. We played the Redskins that day and won, by the way.

It's been an incredible ride since then. We were the first couple ever to be honored by the Pro Football Hall of Fame as members of the Visa Hall of Fans.

Our whole world revolves around being Seahawks fans. Our house is painted in Seahawks colors. Inside, there's not a square inch on any wall, in any room, that's not dedicated to the Seahawks. It's all different eras. In our closet, everything we wear is Seahawks, even shoes and socks, everything. There's no color red in the house. Our Christmas tree has around $4,000.00 worth of Seahawks ornaments. Even our cats are named Replay and End Zone.

On game day, it takes about five hours to get us both ready. For a 1:15 p.m. game, Dede gets up at 2:30 a.m. and paints herself, then me, in order to get to the stadium by 9 a.m. for various events.

We're so honored to represent the Seahawks and all of the fans in the stadium. We are all one big family."

— "Mr. and Mrs. Seahawk,"
  Jeff and Dede Schumaier, Seahawks superfans

" We are grateful to be playing in front of a fan base like the 12s, there is nothing like it."

— Doug Baldwin,
   Seahawks wide receiver

" There are no fans like the 12s. They can't be matched in how loud they get and the energy they bring. It's hard to describe the feeling you get when you step onto the field. If you've never been to a game at CenturyLink, you have to go. It's one of those bucket list things."

— Russell Wilson,
Seahawks quarterback

" Seattle was known for 'the wave' in the '80s. To me, the wave was very effective. It was disruptive, it was loud, it was crazy. From a player's perspective it was great to be a part of.

The Seahawks fans are extremely smart about when to do certain things. They know when to get loud and when to keep quiet. And that's extremely important during the game. It made us feel appreciated while letting our fans participate in the game. The wave was our version of the 12s."

— Curt Warner,
 Former Seahawks All-Pro
 running back; Seahawks
 Ring of Honor, 1994

" To honor their fans, Seahawks management in 1984 retired the No. 12 jersey. In 2003, the 12s earned a flag and a pole at CenturyLink Field. For the past 10 years, opponents have committed 80 false-start penalties, most in the NFL. Having traveled to all the other markets, I'm persuaded Seattle fans are the most committed in the country. In fact, opposing players wish most of those fans were committed."

— Art Thiel,
  Former sports columnist for
  The Seattle Post-Intelligencer
  and co-founder of
  Sportspress Northwest

"The Seahawks fans are game changers. There's nothing worse for the opposing team than to come into our stadium already worried about the fan noise. The noise took their mind off of the game. I can remember Mickey Marvin of the Raiders having tape on his ears inside his helmet to try and block out as much noise as he could. It gave them one more thing to think about. And if it disrupted the opposing team during the game, that was even better."

— Joe Nash,
Former Seahawks All-Pro defensive lineman

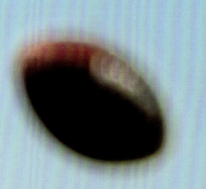

" The 12s are definitely the loudest fans in the NFL, both at home and on the road."

— Jermaine Kearse,
Seahawks
wide receiver

" The 12 helped me to fully realize my passion for the wonderful game I was blessed enough to play and who it was played for. It wasn't just for our team. It was for the whole city, the entire state, the greater Northwest—for everyone who is a 12 or a Seahawks fan. It's a family affair."

— Dave Krieg,
Former Seahawks quarterback;
Seahawks Ring of Honor, 2004

" The passion of the fans, the comradery with the fans—everyone is your brother. You're high-fiving and hooping and hollering with everybody. You're giving hugs to people you don't even know. Especially when you're winning the big games.

To be a part of the 12s is like a church, it's like a family. It's kind of hard to not want to be a part of that. It's like being with 66,000 of your closest friends. It's a brotherhood, it's a sisterhood."

— Lorin "Big Lo" Sandretzky,
 Seahawks superfan

ABOUT THE PICTURES
2014-2015: A YEAR WITH THE 12
Photographs by Robin Layton

For the Seahawks and their fans, the 2014-2015 season will never be forgotten. It began with a celebration of the team's first world championship and ended with a return trip to the Super Bowl. Along the way, the 12s had plenty to howl about, including a miraculous win for the ages in the NFC Championship Game.

FRONT/BACK COVER: Fans cheer on the Seahawks as they beat Green Bay in overtime at CenturyLink Field in Seattle, WA winning the NFC Championship on Jan. 18, 2015. Seahawks 28, Packers 22

INSIDE FRONT COVER: Invited onto the field at CenturyLink Field, select 12s cheer alongside Sea Gals as the Seahawks take the field before the game against St. Louis in on Dec. 28, 2014. Seahawks 20, Rams 6

PAGE 2: Super Bowl Fan Fest at Chase Field (home of the Arizona Diamondbacks) in Phoenix, Arizona at Super Bowl XLIX on Jan. 31, 2015.

PAGE 5: Super Bowl XLVIII victory parade, downtown Seattle, WA on Feb. 15, 2015.

PAGE 6-7: Plane pulling a 12 flag flies over Seahawks Blue Friday Rally at Renton City Hall, Renton, WA on Jan. 9, 2015.

PAGE 8-11: Fans, reflected in puddles as they walk outside CenturyLink Field, arrive for the Seattle-New York Giants game on Nov. 9, 2014. Seahawks 38, Giants 17

PAGE 12-13: The Blue Thunder drum corps gets fans revved up before the Seattle-New York Giants game at CenturyLink Field on Nov. 9, 2014. Seahawks 38, Giants 17

PAGE 14-23: Reflected in puddles outside CenturyLink Field, fans arrive for the Seattle-New York Giants game on Nov. 9, 2014. Seahawks 38, Giants 17

PAGE 24-25: Seahawks Blue Friday Rally at Renton City Hall, Renton, WA on Jan. 9, 2015.

PAGE 26-27: Fans outside CenturyLink Field arrive for the Seattle-San Francisco game on Dec. 14, 2014. Seahawks 17, 49ers 7

PAGE 28-29: Fans arrive early at CenturyLink Field for the Seattle-Oakland game on Nov. 2, 2014. Seahawks 30, Raiders 24

PAGE 30-31: A pair of Seahawks fans are the first to arrive at CenturyLink Field hours before the Seattle-Dallas game on Oct. 12, 2014. Cowboys 30, Seahawks 23

PAGE 32-33: Seahawks practice before their home-opening game against Green Bay at CenturyLink Field on Sept. 4, 2014. Seahawks 36, Packers 16

PAGE 34-35: Sea Gals cheer at the 2014 opening home game at CenturyLink Field on Sept. 4, 2014. Seahawks 36, Packers 16

PAGE 36-37: Fans at the home opener between Seattle and Green Bay at CenturyLink Field on Sept. 4, 2014. Seahawks 36, Packers 16

PAGE 38-39: A man waves a 12 flag on an overpass over Interstate 5 in SeaTac, WA, cheering on the Seahawks as they leave for Super Bowl XLVIII at MetLife Stadium in East Rutherford, NJ on Jan. 26, 2014.

PAGE 40-41: Seahawks fans in the 206 section at CenturyLink Field watch the Seattle-Arizona game on Nov. 23, 2014. Seahawks 19, Cardinals 13

PAGE 42-43: Fans cheer inside CenturyLink Field at the Seattle-New York Giants game on Nov. 9, 2014. Seahawks 38, Giants 17

PAGE 44-45: Fans cheer for the Seahawks at the NFC Championship Game between Seattle and Green Bay at CenturyLink Field on Jan. 18, 2015. Seahawks 28, Packers 22

PAGE 46-47: Invited onto the field at CenturyLink, select 12s cheer alongside Sea Gals as the Seahawks take the field before the game against St. Louis on Dec. 28, 2014. Seahawks 20, Rams 6

PAGE 48-49: Seahawks players wait to run out onto CenturyLink field for the Dec. 28, 2014 regular-season finale against St. Louis. Seahawks 20, Rams 6

PAGE 50-51: Seahawks run onto the field at CenturyLink before the Dallas game on Oct. 12, 2014. Cowboys 30, Seahawks 23

PAGE 52-53:	Seahawks players enter CenturyLink Field for the 2014 NFC Championship Game against the Green Bay Packers on Jan. 18, 2015. Seahawks 28, Packers 22
PAGE 54-55:	Honoring a proud tradition, Seahawks charge onto the field behind the 12 flag prior to the Dallas game at CenturyLink Field on Oct. 12, 2014. Cowboys 30, Seahawks 23
PAGE 56-57:	Seattle vs. New York Giants at CenturyLink Field on Nov. 9, 2014. Seahawks 38, Giants 17
PAGE 58-59:	Sea Gals cheer on the Seahawks during the Denver game at CenturyLink Field on Sept. 21, 2014. Seahawks 26, Broncos 20
PAGE 60-63:	Fans along the sideline cheer the Seahawks as they take the field to play Denver at CenturyLink Field on Sept. 21, 2014. Seahawks 26, Broncos 20
PAGE 64-65:	Seahawks fans fill the stands at CenturyLink Field before the game against San Francisco on Dec. 14, 2014. Seahawks 17, 49ers 7
PAGE 66-67:	Seattle vs. New York Giants at CenturyLink Field on Nov. 9, 2014. Seahawks 38, Giants 17
PAGE 68-69:	Seattle vs. Arizona at CenturyLink Field on Nov. 23, 2014. Seahawks 19, Cardinals 13
PAGE 70-71:	Fans cheer on the Seahawks during the New York Giants game at CenturyLink Field on Nov. 9, 2014. Seahawks 38, Giants 17
PAGE 72-73:	Seattle beats Green Bay in overtime at CenturyLink Field, winning the 2014 NFC Championship on Jan.18, 2015. Seahawks 28, Packers 22
PAGE 74-75:	Seattle vs. San Francisco at CenturyLink Field on Dec. 14, 2014. Seahawks 17, 49ers 7
PAGE 76-77:	Fans cheer on the Seahawks as they beat Green Bay in overtime at CenturyLink Field, winning the NFC Championship on Jan.18, 2015. Seahawks 28, Packers 22
PAGE 78-79:	Sea Gals cheer before the Dallas game at CenturyLink Field on Oct. 12, 2014. They wear pink to support Breast Cancer Awareness Month. Cowboys 30, Seahawks 23
PAGE 80-81:	Seattle vs. Arizona at CenturyLink Field on Nov. 23, 2014. Seahawks 19, Cardinals 13
PAGE 82-83:	A referee signals he is ready to go during the Seattle-St. Louis game at CenturyLink Field on Dec. 28, 2014. Seahawks 20, St. Louis 6
PAGE 84-85:	Seahawks beat the Green Bay Packers in overtime to win the NFC Championship Game on Jan. 18th, 2015. Seahawks 28, Packers 22
PAGE 86-87:	Seattle holds off Oakland at CenturyLink Field on Nov. 2, 2014. Seahawks 30, Raiders 24
PAGE 88-89:	Fans cheer on the Seahawks as they beat Green Bay in overtime at CenturyLink Field, winning the NFC Championship on Jan.18, 2015. Seahawks 28, Packers 22
PAGE 90-93:	Seattle plays Green Bay in the NFC Championship Game at CenturyLink Field on Jan. 18, 2015. Seahawks 28, Packers 22
PAGE 94-97:	Seattle vs. San Francisco at CenturyLink Field on Dec. 14, 2014. Seahawks 17, 49ers 7
PAGE 98-99:	Fans cheer on the Seahawks as they beat Green Bay in overtime at CenturyLink Field, winning the NFC Championship on Jan.18, 2015. Seahawks 28, Packers 22
PAGE 100-101:	A referee gets ready for another play during the Sept. 21, 2014 game against Denver at CenturyLink Field. Seahawks 26, Broncos 20
PAGE 102-103:	A referee signals a Seahawks touchdown during the Oct. 12, 2014 game against Dallas at CenturyLink Field. Cowboys 30, Seahawks 23
PAGE 104-105:	Seattle vs. Green Bay in the NFC Championship Game at CenturyLink Field on Jan. 18, 2015. Seahawks 28, Packers 22
PAGE 106-107:	Mama Blue, a longtime fan and season-ticket holder, cheers on the Seahawks from her end zone seat as Seattle battles the New York Giants on Nov. 9, 2014 at CenturyLink Field. Seahawks 38, Giants 17
PAGE 108-109:	Fans endure the rain at the Seattle-Oakland game at CenturyLink Field on Nov. 2, 2014. Seahawks 30, Raiders 24
PAGE 110-113:	Seattle vs. New York Giants at CenturyLink Field on Nov. 9, 2014. Seahawks 38, Giants 17
PAGE 114-115:	A referee officiates during Seattle's game against Dallas at CenturyLink Field on October 12, 2014. Cowboys 30, Seahawks 23
PAGE 116-117:	Seattle beats Green Bay in overtime to repeat as NFC Champions on Jan. 18, 2015. Seahawks 28, Packers 22

PAGE 118-119:	Seattle-San Francisco at CenturyLink Field on Dec. 14. Seahawks 17, 49ers 7
PAGE 120-121:	Seahawks players wait to run out onto CenturyLink field in Seattle, WA for the Dec. 28, 2014 regular-season finale against St. Louis. Seahawks 20, Rams 6
PAGE 122-123:	A sideline official signals first down at Century Link Field during the Seattle-Arizona game on Nov. 23, 2014. Seahawks 19, Cardinals 3
PAGE 124-125:	Fans celebrate another Seahawks first down against Denver at CenturyLink Field on Sept. 21, 2014. Seahawks 26, Broncos 20
PAGE 126-127:	Seattle gets ready for another play during the Sept. 21, 2014 game against Denver at CenturyLink Field. Seahawks 26, Broncos 20
PAGE 128-129:	Sideline officials signal second down during the Seattle-Dallas game at CenturyLink Field on Oct. 12, 2014. Cowboys 30, Seahawks 23
PAGE 130-131:	A squad of fans cheers alongside the Sea Gals as Seattle takes the field for the regular-season finale at CenturyLink Field on Dec. 28, 2014. Seahawks 20, St. Louis 6
PAGE 132-134:	Seattle vs. Dallas at CenturyLink Field on Oct. 12, 2014. Cowboys 30, Seahawks 23
PAGE 134-135:	Third down, Seattle vs. Dallas at CenturyLink Field on Oct. 12, 2014. Cowboys 30, Seahawks 23
PAGE 136-137:	Seahawks practice at Virginia Mason Athletic Center (VMAC) in Renton, WA on June 2, 2014.
PAGE 138-139:	Seattle vs. Oakland at CenturyLink Field on Nov. 2, 2014. Seahawks 30, Raiders 24
PAGE 140-141:	Fans are loud and proud at Seattle's regular-season finale on Dec. 28, 2014 at CenturyLink Field. Seahawks 20, St. Louis 6
PAGE 142-143:	Touchdown Seahawks! Seattle beats Oakland in their Nov. 2, 2014 game at CenturyLink Field. Seahawks 30, Raiders 24
PAGE 144-145:	Fans cheer at CenturyLink Field as the Seahawks close out the regular season, beating the St. Louis Cardinals on Dec. 28, 2014. Seahawks 20, St. Louis 6
PAGE 146-147:	Seahawks take on the New York Giants at CenturyLink Field on Nov. 9, 2014. Seahawks 38, Giants 17
PAGE 148-149:	Sea Gals cheer before the Dallas game at CenturyLink Field on Oct. 12, 2014. They wear pink to support Breast Cancer Awareness Month. Cowboys 30, Seahawks 23
PAGE 150-151:	Confetti is released after the Seahawks beat the Green Bay Packers in overtime to win the NFC Championship Game on Jan. 18th, 2015. Seahawks 28, Packers 22
PAGE 152-153:	Invited onto the field at CenturyLink Field, select 12s cheer alongside Sea Gals as the Seahawks take the field before the game starts against St. Louis on Dec. 28, 2014. Seahawks 20, Rams 6
PAGE 154-155:	Seahawks fans celebrate the season-opening win against Green Bay on Sept. 4, 2014 at CenturyLink Field. Seahawks 36, Packers 16
PAGE 156-163:	Super Bowl XLVIII victory parade in downtown Seattle, WA on Feb. 15, 2014.
PAGE 164-167:	Seahawks Blue Friday Rally at Renton City Hall, Renton, WA on Jan. 9, 2015.
PAGE 168-169:	Fans cheering on the Seahawks in SeaTac, WA as they leave for Super Bowl XLIX at University of Phoenix Stadium in Glendale, AZ on January 25th, 2015.
PAGE 170-171:	A 12 flag flies proudly during the Super Bowl XLVIII victory parade in Seattle, WA on Feb. 15, 2014.
PAGE 172-173:	CenturyLink Field in Seattle, WA, home of the Seattle Seahawks.
PAGE 174-175:	A Common Wealth Partners team spends more than four hours opening and closing 1,200 window shades to illuminate the Russell Investments Center building with an 18-story 12 in support of the Seahawks.
INSIDE BACK COVER:	Fans proudly wave their 12 flags during Blue Friday Rally at Westlake Park on Jan. 16th, 2015 to prepare for the NFC Championship Game at CenturyLink Field against Green Bay on Jan. 18th.

ABOUT THE AUTHOR

ROBIN LAYTON
photojournalist/artist/filmmaker

During her 25 years as a photojournalist, renowned photographer Robin Layton has produced countless notable photographs and earned a place among the world's top photographers. By age 24, she was honored by **LIFE** magazine as one of the eight most talented photographers in America. In 1991, her image of a young departing soldier, embracing his daughter on the USS *John F. Kennedy,* was used globally in ads for AT&T and the USO and was on the cover of **LIFE** magazine's "The Year in Pictures" issue. Her photo story on runaway teens in downtown Seattle was nominated for a **Pulitzer Prize**. Sports enthusiasts will remember her iconic photograph of Ken Griffey Jr. from the 1995 American League playoffs ("The Smile at the Bottom of the Pile"). She has been a **Nikon Ambassador** since 2013.

After an award-winning career at five newspapers, including staff positions with the *Virginian-Pilot* and the *Seattle Post-Intelligencer*, Robin embarked on a freelance career that has taken her on assignments around the world. Along the way, she has photographed everyone from prom queens to actual kings, street people to presidents, and personalities from Jennifer Aniston to Oprah Winfrey. She has also expanded the boundaries of traditional photography, combining her images with vintage found objects to create critically acclaimed and highly sought art pieces.

What pictures do best is capture a moment in time. Robin's work illuminates the life within that moment. She compels you to take a second look, a new view of the world around us.

ROBIN'S OTHER BOOKS
hoop: the american dream, powerHouse books
A Letter To My Dog, Chronicle books

ARTIST STATEMENT

photo by Anthony Bolante

Everything about Seattle and the Northwest inspires me and my work. I am home here. I've found my spot in the world. I love this beautiful, magical city of ours. From the day I moved here, it felt like the city was pulling art out of me that I didn't even know I had.

The connection I have with Seattle sports began shortly after I moved here. I had the privilege of taking the iconic photo of Ken Griffey Jr., "The Smile at the Bottom of the Pile," when the Mariners won the AL West Championship in 1995. That's when I first felt the power of Seattle fans to lift their team.

I've witnessed that same power time and again over the past years at CenturyLink Field. The deafening devotion of Seahawks fans provided a perfect subject for this book. I wanted to capture the energy and spirit of the 12s and elevate that passion to high art.

As I think about it more, I realize that the Seahawks blue and green colors represent the breathtaking power of the water and trees that surround and define us. Our Seahawks also represent the strength, perseverance, and spirit of our beautiful, sparkling city. We are 12!

— Robin Layton

ACKNOWLEDGEMENTS

My "12" artwork and this book would not have been possible without the following people:

Laura Vecsey: This book started with you. Thank you for your friendship all these years and for your generosity in taking me to a Seahawks practice.

Peter McLoughlin: Thank you for supporting this project from the very beginning. This collection of images would never have happened without you. I am forever grateful.

Kelly McLoughlin: Thank you for believing in my artwork and for all your enthusiasm, support and wonderful ideas surrounding it. I am overwhelmed by your kindness and generosity.

Julie Barber: Thank you from the bottom of my heart for all the opportunities you provided so I could capture my artwork. My eternal gratitude for your help with this book. You are an angel that came into my life.

Jeff Richards: Thank you for all your time, patience and knowledge, and for being my guiding light throughout the process of creating my art exhibits and this book.

Doug Orwiler: Thanks for being so wonderful and easy to work with and for helping make this book happen.

Amy Sprangers: You are a bright light! Thanks for the amazing opportunity to exhibit my artwork at CenturyLink Field! A dream come true.

Courtney Haeg: Thank you so much for all your help with my "12" artwork exhibit at CenturyLink Field. You are a delight to work with.

John Weaver, Ed Goines, Becca Rollins: Thank you for helping me with this book! I so appreciate each of you for meeting with me and for taking the time to view my work.

Special thanks to Lane Gammel and Rich Gonzales for their help with quotes for this book.

Alicia Nickell: Thanks for all your enthusiasm and help with this book.

Stacey Winston: Thank you for your enthusiasm and support for my artwork from the very beginning. I am so very honored to exhibit at Winston Wachter Fine Art Gallery.

Judith, Jessica, Anna: Thank you for all your help with my "12" artwork. You are all simply wonderful to work with!

Billy O'Neill: Thank you for your generousity and huge heart. I so appreciate your help with this book.

Thank you to all the Seahawks alumni who gave me quotes and stories for this book: Kenny Easley, Dave Krieg, Steve Largent, Joe Nash and Curt Warner.

Thank you to Coach Carroll and all the current Seahawks players who gave me quotes and for this book: Doug Baldwin, Jermaine Kearse, Jon Ryan and Russell Wilson.

Special thanks to Steve Raible and Art Thiel for your quotes in this book.

Thank you to all the Seahawks superfans who gave me their quotes and stories for this book:

"Big Lo"
Lorin Sandretzky

"Bernie Hawk"
Paul Gates

"Mama Blue"
Patti Hammond

"Mr. and Mrs. Seahawk"
Jeff & Dede Schumaier

"Kiltman"
Neil Hart

Kim and David: I truly don't know what I'd do without you both. You are not only extremely talented but are extremely generous with huge hearts. We are family.

Shakti: Thanks for always believing in me and supporting me in everything I do. I love you.

To my parents, Shirley and Barrett Crump: Everything I do, I do to honor you. Thank you for always believing in me and encouraging me to always follow my dreams.

And thank you to all the 12s. This book is for you.

Photographs © 2015 Robin Layton
Forward © Steve Largent

All rights reserved. No part of this book may be reproduced in any manner in any media, or transmitted by any means whatsoever, electronic or mechanical (including photocopy, film or video recording, Internet posting, or any other information storage and retrieval system), without the prior written permission of Robin Layton.

First edition, 2015

ISBN: 978-0-615-48458-7

Book Design by Kim Carney, David Miller and Robin Layton.

Photos of Super fans courtesy of Seattle Seahawks.

To order original artwork from this book or to see more of Robin's work, visit her websites:

robinlayton.com
12robinlayton.com
hooptheamericandream.com